Swan ...mmer

Swan Hammer

An Instructor's Guide to Mirrors

POEMS BY **MAGGIE GRABER**

WHEELBARROW BOOKS ▪ *East Lansing, Michigan*

Wheelbarrow Books
Michigan State University Press
East Lansing, Michigan 48823-5245

Michigan State University Press
East Lansing, Michigan 48823-5245

Library of Congress Control Number: 2021945069

ISBN 978-1-61186-431-1 (paper)
ISBN 978-1-60917-700-3 (PDF)
ISBN 978-1-62895-468-5 (ePub)
ISBN 978-1-62896-462-2 (Kindle)

Cover design by Erin Kirk
Cover art: vvvita (Adobe stock)

Visit Michigan State University Press at *www.msupress.org*

With the publication of Maggie Graber's collection of poems, *Swan Hammer: An Instructor's Guide to Mirrors*, the Residential College in the Arts and Humanities (RCAH) Center for Poetry at Michigan State University offers its tenth book in our Wheelbarrow Books Poetry Series. Clearly, we pay homage to William Carlos Williams and his iconic poem, "The Red Wheelbarrow." Readers will remember the poem begins "so much depends upon . . ." that red wheelbarrow.

For many of us, so much depends upon the wonderful collections of poetry we can find to help us in times of crisis. As we find ourselves in mid-2021, hopefully nearing the end of a COVID-19 global pandemic with over 620,000 deaths in this country alone, it is a comfort that Maggie Graber gives us a book of poems that acknowledges our need for connections, for relationships with people and the natural world, and that moves away from a "monogamous bond between me and my screen" ("iContact / Screens"). What a joyous and spunky book to encounter in these times. I never knew when I left one poem behind what was coming in the next one. The stories Graber tells and the language she uses are crisp and imaginative. I trust the honesty of her voice. How many times did I find myself saying about a line, "What an incredible juxtaposition of ideas and language." The poet seems to take on these poems with ease. They seem effortless, the mark of real skill. What is it that holds this manuscript with such diverse titles as "Tomato Prayer," "Getting Lost in Gary, Indiana," "Why I Shouldn't Be an FBI Special Agent," and "Ode to The Weather Channel" together? It's the poet's voice, the diction and detail, the imagery and tone, that draws us into the small worlds she creates on the page.

When I first picked up *Swan Hammer*, I felt the collection would be totally wonderful or a compete jumble of disconnects. My first response was correct. The collection is quirky and full of surprises. I love it. I want to quote part of the second poem in the collection, "The Poet Dreams of Levitation," as an indication of why I knew early on that this manuscript might be a winner:

My poems would love / to light your door / on a summer night. / My poems / aren't policy. My poems / aren't property. I promise / I've never written a poem / in your backyard / while you were out / shopping for furniture / but I can tell you / a poem is like a backyard / or a patio or a porch / or a stoop / or a fire escape / or a roof or wherever / your immediate surroundings / extend, you / are a poem . . .

How could I not keep reading? Won't you?

At the end of this poem, the poet imagines a world where everyone is writing poems:

For days and days and days / until the days equal / one week / and that is one week / of people / writing poems / seven days / all over the planet / our human species / in quiet fever / not / hurting / anyone

Let us beat our swords into plowshares. Let us trade in our pistols for poems. Let everyone pick up a pen (yes, a pen, not a computer), a blank paper, and this book of poems. Let us create, and not destroy.

As our number of Wheelbarrow Books publications increases, we hope that our audience increases also. Help us spread the word. In the beginning was the word, and the word became the poem. So much depends upon the collaboration of reader, writer, and poem, the intimate ways we come to know one another. Poet Edward Hirsch tells us that a poem is one solitude speaking to another. So much depends upon this continuing relationship.

—ANITA SKEEN, *Wheelbarrow Books Series Editor*

Swan Hammer: An Instructor's Guide to Mirrors exposes the collision and coexistence of popular culture, sexual identity, the natural world, virtual reality, families, and the cosmos. There is a sonnet in the collection, there is humor, intimacy, there are odes and elegies, a poem called "Pi Day." There is fluidity in time and space and voice. There is great pleasure and pain on these pages.

The title poem, "swan hammer" appears last. It is a short poem, no caps, and rounds out the collection very well. The swan here is made of paper, and the hammer beats inside the body of the narrator. Here are the final lines:

before sleep
the girl inside me
hammers the wall
of my skull

light rides in
on a wave
of flat paper swans

she folds one
she folds another

she's trying to tell me
she knows the way out

"Day 1, December 22, 2012" begins in an Italian restaurant in the first moments of the Mayan Apocalypse and moves us past a brother dancing in the snow, and then to a Solstice ritual in a tacky apartment. We feel painful confusion over sexual identity, secrets kept, and a hopeful desire for acceptance. Toward the end three sets of numbers representing a sudoku puzzle are inserted into the text. Could our lives be reduced to a simple Japanese numbers game? One solution, one way to be.

The subtitle comes from "Roller Derby Night in Southern Illinois." Strong skaters with *agency* skate slowly and deliberately round and round the oval rink. A poem written to someone gone. There is so much longing, and the poem ends with a final wish:

> and I wish, on the way home, you could have seen
> the Big Dipper above Crab Orchard Lake, nailed
> to the dark wall of space, the moon spinning slow,
> flashing on the water like aluminum foil,
> like an instructor's guide to mirrors.

"Poem for Ms. Frizzle" is for the teacher who could plunge her students into the ocean, or the human body. She could blast them to outer space and burrow them down to the core of the earth. This is a poem of love for Ms. Frizzle and Kate McKinnon, the voice of Ms. Frizzle in the cartoon.

> Ms. Frizzle—and maybe I am talking
> to McKinnon now—I think I love you. Could
>
> love you. I know it's silly, you're a cartoon. Maybe
> I just wish to hover above a sound wave,
>
> a lunar crater, a rainforest. Maybe I wish my limbs
> would convert into wind-blown seeds . . .

There are so many things I love about this collection. I love how "I remember Nashville, the dueling piano bar" is not an homage to music, and how in "At the Twilight of the Big Bang," it might be time for a new origin story. I love the way the poems look on the page. I love the honesty and vulnerability of this collection.

—SARAH BAGBY

for my family, my teachers, and anyone who could use this

Contents

Said the river: imagine everything you can imagine, then keep on going.

—MARY OLIVER

Self-Portrait as Hammer

The grip is everything.
Then the swing-back
and journey down,
song of steel
forged in a forge.
Let me do the work.
The marriage
between the body
and the tool,
the way I bend gravity
in your hand. Before
I could build
anything, I had to learn
what God gave me:
bag full of nails,
the stone
my body becomes
in thought.
Look at the nail
planted like a stem—
what we can build
and take apart.
To make a bird,
you need two birds.
To make a hammer, you need
another hammer, fire,
and a handle long
as a neck. Otherwise,
you got no song.

1

The Poet Dreams of Levitation

Who are my enemies? / Sufjan Stevens / is not my enemy. / The letter "y" certainly / is not my enemy. / I even lift my arms / and make the shape / of the letter / with my body. / Once / it was suggested / I not use / ampersands / in my poems / and as much as I'd like to / I still hear / that voice and see / when I close my eyes / the mustache / attached to it. / I *do* like a sentence. / My poems / are my puppets. / I like that sentence. / My poems / are my puppets / and my poems / feel sad / because my poems / would love / to be plants / or music / or light. / My poems would love / to light your door / on a summer night. / My poems / aren't policy. My poems / aren't property. I promise / I've never written a poem / in your backyard / while you were out / shopping for furniture / but I can tell you / a poem is like a backyard / or a patio or a porch / or a stoop / or a fire escape / or a roof or wherever / your immediate surroundings / extend, you / are a poem too / and if you have a backyard / and like to spend time there / I love that for you. / If you like to go outside / at all, we / are on the same page. / If you don't / we are both still here / on this page, so / I try to avoid / tragedy, but I woke / on Earth today / and I wanted to talk / about ampersands / then I strayed / and the point seems, well / meh. Even if I told you / I wouldn't feel it / in the same way / you know? / I had this grand vision. / I talked about the word / "and" / the three letters / that constitute / its sound / the lineage of alphabets / how history / just goes back / in time / then I started thinking / about time / and couldn't help / but think / of space. Then I imagined / a world / where everyone / wrote poems. This / is a space I go / in myself / when I need to feel / grounded in the world / I'd like to live. / It's a good example / of an ice-breaker question / I'd answer / or a Happy Thought I'd think / if a fairy flew through the window / right now / and communicated via / emphatic facial gestures / she was taking me / to Neverland. / Everyone on Earth / writing poems. / Just that. / My feet / lifting off the floor. / For days and days and days / until the days equal / one week / and that is one week / of people / writing poems / seven days / all over the planet / our human species / in quiet fever / not / hurting / anyone

Pi Day

Today, in honor of Pi Day, a day
that falls on Albert Einstein's birthday,
when all the crows outside
my window fly in circles rather
than in straight lines, when time
won't stop for anyone but breathes
more deeply at 9:26:53 a.m.
and p.m., when the middle school
math teachers bake two cherry pies
for their students because
they "r" squared, this day in the middle
of March, the plowed snow taking longest
to melt, the coffee ring from my mug
on the table like the clean halo
of a calculator, when every tire
and hubcap sings praise to the shape
of their form, this holy day of numbers,
the Greek letter like an end table
in every equation or a doorway
to another dimension where graph paper
is the only flag we'll ever need, today
if it is mathematically possible, I would like
to exist in the realm of pure ideas
where I can drift from quadrant
to quadrant playing basketball and eating pizza
or drawing circles with my finger
onto the air space in front of me, saying this
is a dog running through a yard
after the stick I frisbeed through the sky,
this is a shell spider, whose hard cream-colored back
catches and reflects moonlight, its body
a lamp in the webbed dark, this
is equality, this

is division, this is a cloud of thought
trailing above me like a train
of kites, this is the abstract concept of weightlessness
in January, whose body I will curve mine into
again one day, this is a Venn diagram
of infinity and decimal places, logic
and lust, brain and pancakes
and teeth, of yesterday and tomorrow
whose common relative
is today—this day—this glorious
hula-hooping day
when where we end and where we begin
may as well be
exactly the same.

The Ghost of Robert Frost Visits

Tonight in my freezer, the voice of Robert Frost
jokes about the differences between
ice cream and shaved ice, which,
he concludes, are profound. Like the Milky Way
trapped within the coiled arms
of a vending machine at a rest stop on I-65
my brain still remembers. Or the satellite that fell
through atmosphere like a dodo, landing
just before sundown in a Texas backyard.
There are choices, he says, and then there are magnetic fields.
Space-time continuums. Wormholes in the night sky
you can make in your kitchen from a used-up roll of paper towel.
Cover the cardboard tube full of comets and stars,
rocket ships blazing fiery trails through dark sky,
leaving behind tails of steel-smoked snow. Feel free, he says,
to toss it in the air like a baton, catching the galactic bridge
behind your back, and lean your eye close
to the red tissue-paper lens you've taped to the tube
so it doubles as a telescope. Feel free to wander
into the alley behind your apartment, tracing the paths
of power lines through autumn with your finger.
I can pretend my clothes are secrets, shedding them
like leaves beneath the stars. Cats
might watch me, with the moon blowing kisses to tides
200,000 miles away, and even though the walruses
tanning themselves on ice shelves don't care about ice cream, if they did
the ghost of Robert Frost tells me they'd prefer strawberry
over vanilla and chocolate, though he wouldn't bet his death on it.
He's noticed many mammals coming around these days
to rainbow-colored snow cones—a trend
no prophet could have predicted, no meteorologist
could have foreseen forming over the Pacific coast.
These are difficult times to be human.

To choose between one coldness and another.
To stain your tongue with any one of a dozen tasty sweetnesses.
Before he disappears to the arctic of my freezer,
I ask him to reveal the most unexpected difference
between life and death—
does the ground smell like turtle shell?
Do souls rise like chimneys?
But he doesn't answer. Through the telescope's red veil,
the moon blushes in the gaze of stars.

Roller Derby Night in Southern Illinois

for Elise

I wish you could have seen the oval track
the girls skated around like a cluster
of orbiting planets, all of them in kneepads
and helmets plastered with stickers, all of us
eating hot dogs, cheering for the sun-colored team

and the little girl no older than four who toed
the out-of-bounds line during introductions
like she was standing at a shoreline, holding out her hand
for high-fives from the girls ducking close to the ground
as they approached her, and how she'd turn, feet

springing off the floor, to look back
at her grandma laughing, the wrinkles in her face
you would have thought beautiful
beneath the umbrella voice of the announcer
as the referee with a full-sleeve tattoo of a skeleton

traced figure eights with his skates like an ad for infinity. And I wish
you could have seen the girls not afraid to wear fishnets
and compete. The girls not afraid to get knocked down
in rainbow-colored, zebra-striped spandex. The girls
not afraid to get bruised and banged up, turn blue

and black if it means there's a place for what's real, what's hard,
and what's gorgeous. I wish you could have seen
the disco ball on the back of a girl's black shorts
and how she tackled one of the MissFits off the track,
green mouth-guard glowing plutonium on her tongue

and I wish, on the way home, you could have seen
the Big Dipper above Crab Orchard Lake, nailed

to the dark wall of space, the moon spinning slow,
flashing on the water like aluminum foil,
like an instructor's guide to mirrors.

Poem for Whomever Hacked My Debit Card and Spent $150 at the Macy's in Alexandria, Virginia

I wonder if guilt snared your mind like a polluted river.
Or if you, a repeat offender, live for the heist.
I can't help but ask. Why Macy's?
Why not max me out at some gas station on slurpees
and breakfast sandwiches, which is the first place
my mind goes so who am I to judge, but really.
How did you spend my money? Disney films
conditioned me to imagine you as a villain—
sinister grin, thunder rumbling laugh—but you're just as likely
somebody's mom in a mini-van driving her kids home
from play practice. Could be some dude into tiki torches?
Maybe you like ballet. What I really want to know
is if you ever imagine the world populated with piranhas.
If you'll live in the penciled shadow of the Washington Monument
until the day you die. You should know,

though you never will, when I was sixteen
my family drove through Virginia on the way to Williamsburg.
That night I fell in love with the word *turnpike*
listening to a CD of classical music, a cantaloupe sunset
in the rear window, as we drove deeper and deeper
into the dark mouth of a thunderstorm.

My dad cursed the rain and windshield wipers
and my mom gripped the seat cushion like a Catholic nun
clutching a crucifix, but it was the first time I felt close
to something holy. The way a mountain can be a kind of saint.
How one day, I could give up everything to know
a life that hinges on the seconds between a flash of light
and the crackling open. It's been years since the rain cleaned
the hard, blue shell of our Dodge Caravan
as we made our way east toward the Atlantic,

and even though you'll never know who I am,
because you spent one hundred and fifty of my dollars at a Macy's,
because this week my life will be filled with one inconvenience
after another, even if Virginia holds no space in the car trunk
of your heart, let me just say I didn't know a road trip
could open a window to another world
until that drive. Did you not sense this too
when you handed the cashier a card with my number?
Could you not feel it when she scanned the items, the store
above you like a mystery, or when the purchase flashed green
on the screen of the register?

                    Wherever you are,
perhaps in the company of your children, maybe
in the living room of the home you've lived in
since the Berlin Wall crumbled like crackers to the ground,
one day your body will putter its last song.

Flute. Harmonica. Bell.

Even if your thumb can no longer tap
the number of beats, understand
it will be the second number
we have to share.

Poem for My Downstairs Neighbor

My third day in the building, you hobbled up the fire escape to tell me.
Dad just dead of a heart attack. Friend murdered over drugs. Your busted
    knee.

Basil grew in a blue tub, a baby's bath by the bike rack. You said take as much
as I wanted, all my hands could carry, but the two capsized boats of your eyes

warned to keep my distance. Months later when I re-signed the lease,
the landlady's son slipping his mother would not rent out to you again—

fights with your girlfriend, bounced rent checks—I wasn't sad, but I wonder
where you will go. If a river exists in this town. If any hands could heal you.

Just this morning you opened your door to the damp smell of earth after
    thunder,
the volume dial of your radio all the way to the end. Blasting a song by Sonny
    and Cher

I imagine reminds you of shag carpet, or what it feels like to be in love, I wrote
on the balcony above you a poem on the speed of light. How it travels like a
    thought

through space. How even the illumination which makes visible the universe
stems from somewhere else. Stars juiced on nuclear fusion. Electrical lines
    flowing

from power plants. A beaded line of luminous orbs strung to a glowworm
on the ceiling of the darkest cave in New Zealand. Like particular species of
    fish

near the ocean's floor, the glowworm knows it must create its own light
to attract insects. The insects have not figured out the light they love

will be used against them, and can you blame them? Every day, the sun
tricks us into thinking light shows us the truth, but last night

before the thunderstorm, a squirrel dug up an acorn it buried months ago.
Hands scooping the dirt, it scampered up an oak tree where I no longer

could see it. When the storm finally showed up, I opened all my windows
to capture it on film—lightning crooked between clouds—but I could never
    predict

when it was about to strike. Atmosphere just right. Electricity in the sky
once believed to be a god. I don't know if you were home

to witness that storm, or if you know where the pine-flavored breeze
will carry you in the approaching months, but for several years

I have wanted a fish tank. Quiet sound of bubbles. Small shipwreck
or Buddha statue on a bed of sand-colored stones. When you leave

I will buy one, along with a few fish. I will change their water
when it needs to be changed. I will scrub the tank's glass walls

until we see each other clearly, fish eye to my eye, and in this act of nurturing,
I will try to learn how we care for other lives. This mutual biology.

How nature helps us remember the world as it was when the continents
were united, when the clouds held the kingdom of Zeus.

Elegy for the Early 21st Century Hipster

Mascot of the Age of Information,
your time has come.
Ask the curator at the Museum
of Social Histories, or
the geologist who loves volcanoes
so much, she'd camp on that lip
of rock to watch a pool of magma
bubble like tomato soup.
Who wouldn't want to return
from logic's ledge, say
they've listened to lava? One day
you will live in a glass case.
One day a graduate student will study
the significance of facial hair and flannel,
earning their PhD after hours
of analyzing how you dressed
yourself in languages
you did not understand
yet no one claimed your name.
You, an existential dilemma.
I wonder if you're already dead.
Wouldn't you have been the first to know?
What dreams did you not share?
Did your neck pulse a bassline
of half notes? Did the sidewalk sewers
sing? Herds of taxicabs painted like tigers,
did the engines purr you to sleep?
No, I've come here like an evangelist
to tell you, except
forget Jesus. Forget how one day
someone will write their dissertation
on the cultural representations of Christ,
drawing parallels between the hipster beard

and a lack of transcendence. No.
Before you go, tell me
the earth's core is 9,800 degrees.
Tell me how you think it feels
to burn that deep.

Dear Los Angeles

I hate white Jesus. I hate the tattoo
of a fidget spinner on the wrist
of a boy on the bus. I hate most of the poems
of narrative ambiguity I've written the last five months.
I hate business suits and belts, every restaurant
still using Styrofoam for leftovers, plastic forks, knives.
I hate this president and the garbage dump of his heart
where nothing decomposes, car doors and strollers rusting
in broad daylight. I hate thinking of metaphors for hate, as if
it was a rodent I could evict from the apartment I don't have.
I hate technically being homeless in this liminal space called thirty
and answering questions about my life or species of lilies
I know nothing about or when people say fish
don't feel pain. I hate guns and short memories
and the Confederate flags I'd see every time
I drove the interstates of Alabama. I hate the patriarchy
and men who don't have that word in their vocabulary.
I hate Jimmy Fallon for rustling 45's hair the same way
he'd pet a golden retriever, and how much
the Minneapolis–St. Paul airport charges me for parking my car
in their garage when I fly across this country for weddings,
and now when I dream, I dream that my eyes close
like garage doors: slow, even, loud enough to hear floors away.
I hate climate change denier message boards,
the internet sometimes, my back when it hurts.
I hate that I haven't learned Spanish yet
or figured out a better way to say
I am covered in music. I hate my bladder
and one day when I'm old,
if I get old, I think I may hate my jaw
which I hate the US health care industry prematurely for,
and also appropriately for, in this year we're calling 2017,
as a guy with an unbuttoned shirt shouts at this Los Angeles bus stop,
   his feet

caked with dirt, his hair knotted like a blanket destined to spend
the rest of its days in and out of a dog's wet mouth—I hate
how his mind has crashed in on itself like a wave,
and Fox News, and the people who think they're thinking when really
they're just repeating something someone said, and though I don't hate
    Wisconsin
where I work right now, it's whiter than a northern winter, which I do
hate, and I hate how bored teens must be
to skateboard and look at their phones simultaneously,
and I hate the unconvincing nature of logic
in our present political discourse and the relevance
of dystopian fiction. Sometimes I want to unzip my neck,
let the bullshit I've tuned out leak from my head. Say,
Take me back to the mechanic. Tell them to loosen the valves, as if
I weren't some organic thing. I hate how I could keep going,
but, dear reader, I don't want to keep you here.
You've made it this far, and though my eyes may not rise
to meet yours under the canopy of this taco stand,

a mural of cacti on this building's side, the cloudless sky,
I remember now, I can count in Spanish to ten.
Uno. I am 2,000 miles away from home.
Dos. I am less than ten blocks from the ocean.
Tres. I hate the floating islands of plastic
swirling in the sea. *Cuatro.* I just read a news story
about two strangers bonding over country music in Las Vegas
before a man fired bullets into the crowd from a hotel room.
Cinco. When it happened, I was in the North Woods
surrounded by birch trees. *Seis.* It can all
be different, #myfavoriteidea. *Siete.* Dear Los Angeles,
I squint one of my garage door eyes to focus. *Ocho.*
I swear—I'm like a pinhole camera at the beginning of its life,
that there's a light pole in my body begging to be built.
Nueve. I hate how far I've come to arrive at the end
of this poem, which began in the northeast
of my hating heart on the Fourth of July
in New York City, my eyes on one fixed point

in the subway after another, water streaming
into the bottomless pits of the Twin Towers, at every flag
a name, the world proving almost impossible
to feel. And one more makes *diez.*
I wonder now, how do we open our hands
to the ground's rising heat, or listen to the pink
and green truths of '8os pop music? How do we look out
from the center of our lives toward the dark
silhouettes of winter trees? Orange sky glowing
like a late-night infomercial. Sun playing hide-and-seek
somewhere else.

I remember Nashville, the dueling piano bar

overlooking Broadway, the loud row
of honky-tonks and bachelorette parties,
where a middle-aged couple from Oregon
sat next to me—a young, lone, woman traveler,
and asked if I was sad. Holding my beer
between my hands, I said, nice as I could,
you don't even know me, thinking how this
is America: country songs and assumptions
about what percentage of people there that night voted
for Trump, and this woman whose bucket list
had on it the Indy 500, an event from my
home state I didn't know people put on bucket lists,
the man put his hand on my back like I was his
daughter, this question they would never
ask a man seated with himself, they never learned
they were chatting with a queer gal, that I love
bright lights and coffee ice cream, I said instead
I was a poet in town for the night en route
to a wedding in Alabama. We bonded over
the Northern California town of Ukiah
with a Buddhist temple where they used to live
and the next town south from the farm where I worked
my twenty-ninth summer. I wondered then as I wonder now:
are you *not* sad? You meaning them, the couple
on vacation, with the immigration laws and dreamers,
that racist, sexist election, this new land
of continual disconnection, do they not sink when
the news tugs their ear lobes, sticks its tongue
inside? Some nights I talk to no one
but children stacking rocks on Lake Superior
while fireworks blast across the water, and I
shouldn't have to tell you that I see the sky
bloom before I hear each *boom*, but I do—see it,

that is, then hear it. Their mother says the rock towers
are called *cairns* and used to help travelers hiking on trails
know they were on the right path. And I don't look up
to tell her, in honest amazement, I had only
just told that to a teenage girl two days before.
Instead I fumble picking up my pen, a lone, young
girl taking notes on fireworks on the day after
the Fourth of July. I don't say anything
except when I notice the ten rock towers this girl
has built—*those are amazing*—and repeat it
when she doesn't hear me—*those are awesome,*
as if the way she stacks it all up just might save us all.

iContact / Screens

I mean disconnection. I mean unplugged.
        I mean technology's phantom
                eyes. Every building a temple to Wi-Fi.
        Hundred apps to the heart. Monogamous

bond between me and my screen. I ride
        a public transit bus through Seattle.
                Watch network names vanish
        like dead. This is me stretching my narrow belt

of mind around words like *genocide* in the twenty-first
        century. I see a friend alive
                in another city, watch them dance,
        dive into snow, but I can't feel

their face. Can't reach out except to finger
        a flat plate of glass, sensitive to touch.

Tomato Prayer

Northern California

Morning of work, morning of wood
in the stove, coffee grounds
like the dark soil of Iowa, I have come
to this farm kitchen to live
beside the bowls of peppers and potatoes,
corn plucked from the rows, boards
and knives that slice the earth made flesh,
and here I apologize, wanderer that I am,
to take another trail and tell you
I don't like the word *flesh*—
how I imagine a cantaloupe crescent
tilled from an arm or thigh,
and if I have run away,
let it be so I can dig
in the dirt to plant myself: fist
of flowers unfurl
on my forehead, watered
with the nightmares of deer.
A bowl of tomatoes burns
like a bonfire, and though
I didn't plan it, maybe this
is a prayer to a god
I've never spoken with
but has watched me each night
the trance of moonlit clouds
calls me like a mouse
to a trap. If this is death, let wakefulness
grant me another name, a sound
I could hide under my tongue
like the black and yellow suits of bees.
Friend, how will you know me
when all I am is wet dirt

underneath your feet? How will we love
when all we've buried grows
on vines and tastes unsalted,
like weakening sun?

Seasonal

In the Midwest, everyone has three hearts.
You can't survive winter without winter
surviving you, so you look like a prayer
on your knees. Snow Shovel Gods, clear us
a path. God of Beer and Snowflakes.
Goddess of Land and Lake Effect.
The first heart is a ball of ice. Blue
baseball. The second, fire.
The third heart pulls in every spring
when the sun cracks you open with a sledgehammer.
Digs like a hound dog for bones. Claws the soil
with fingered teeth, and like a midwife
plucks a newborn from a clot of brown dirt.
Fresh stems from the cold, wet March of you.

Getting Lost in Gary, Indiana

Nothing I could have done about the outdated map
of Northwest Indiana my dad handed me in our driveway
as he said, *Here Mag*, placing it like a pumpkin
in my palm. *You're gonna wanna use this*

if you get lost. Nothing I could have said either to the interstate
construction, stick figures digging on orange signs
warning drivers of roadwork. Beneath gray clouds
billowing from steel mill towers. Underneath the white sun

casting shadows of airplanes on the lake. Days earlier,
the manager of the ice cream parlor where I worked pouring
batter into waffle irons in high school gave me four tickets
to a Gary RailCats minor league baseball game.

With three friends in my red Cavalier, we drove
the thirty-five minutes from Valparaiso into Gary
and missed our exit in a river of two-lane traffic
when a semi blocked our route to the stadium.

The next two exits after that no longer existed
so we kept driving, into the city's center where steam rose
from sewers like the spirits of men taken by assembly lines,
and blue city flags hung, heads down, in the wind.

For years I had heard people say not to find yourself in Gary,
a city once notched in the Factory Belt of America
now a rusted Mustang on cinder blocks in the driveway.
This city that welcomed immigrants from Italy,

Greece, Poland, Russia, the Balkans, Ireland, Germany
to its steel shoreline. This city greeting its iron handshake
to 9,000 Mexicans by the 1930s, and a wave of African Americans
coming from the South in the Great Migration. This city once dubbed

the "Magic City." Who birthed the Jackson 5, Janet, the King of Pop.
A city rooted in The Region, that corner pocket of Indiana
that is not Indiana, where Chicago overflows the Illinois border
carrying a legacy of White Flight. The city now left

for dead. Streets lined with abandoned grocery stores, theaters,
cathedrals where now only pigeons come to pray.
Hooded stoplights, auditoriums, the empty swimming pool
at the Sheraton Hotel the earth has started to reclaim—

we drove those streets looking for a baseball stadium
and listening for gunshots. Four out of place suburban white kids.
What did we know about decay? About the ghost of history
whose breath smells like freight trains in winter,

whose skin flakes like paint off a Laundromat door.
When we figured out where we were supposed to turn,
my car like a rash on the road, I turned the wrong way
down a one-way street toward four lanes of traffic

and a blue Cadillac in my lane that did not slow down,
that wanted, I think, to see if I would turn away first,
which I did, onto another one-way in the wrong direction,
onto a street with a boarded-up drug store,

brick wall mural of the Jackson 5,
newspaper stands and front page of *The Times*,
and on a billboard—
                    City of the Century,
100 Years—the People of Gary Welcome You.

Day 1, December 22, 2012

I was there when the Mayan Apocalypse began
in the dining room of an Italian restaurant,
Bing Crosby crooning "I'll be home for Christmas"
through the speakers, and me watching my mother

amid the smells of pesto and marinara
remember her father, dead two and a half years.
While families in Indiana and around the Midwest
counted down to midnight when they finally

would meet God, I stood to hug her, whispered
I love you, as if a voice could glue back together
the bits of Belleek Irish porcelain
buried in the graveyard of a heart. After dinner,

my brother dancing in the parking lot, snow falling
like bleached confetti, I drove the ten minutes
down Campbell Street in silence to an old friend's Solstice party.
Ate carrot sticks and pretzels under palm trees

in her Margaritaville basement, and when everyone
left, we kneeled on the floor, offering
dead birds, two fistfuls of feathers, to winter ritual.
In college an ex-boyfriend strangled her.

Nails in her neck, stage curtain beginning to fall, her father
flashed in her mind and she punched the guy in the jaw.
In college I once fell in love with a boy and a girl
at the same time, though it would take six years

to collapse the scaffolding rusting around my heart
so I could tell a truth so plain.
Next morning at the kitchen table, sunlight spilling
through the window, I didn't tell my mother

the text message I had just received
containing a little heart was from a girl
I couldn't stop thinking about. Instead
I watched her nurse a headache. Navigate

a Sudoku puzzle. When she finished, I held it to the light
like I was deciphering code:

7 / 3 / 1   6 / 5 / 8   2 / 4 / 9
6 / 9 / 2   1 / 3 / 4   5 / 8 / 7
8 / 5 / 4   2 / 9 / 7   1 / 3 / 6

Months later, I'd hinge open the rusted mouth of a mailbox,
let the postal service deliver what I could not say aloud.

When Grandpa Murphy fought in the war,
she said, *he cracked codes for the Allies.*
At war's end, with Europe avalanched
in concrete, there was nothing else to do
but build it once again.

Margaret

When you're named after your mother's
greatest heartbreak, your name
her mother's name, the same letters
in the same order, the same touch
of lips at the beginning of the word, *Mmm*,
as if it tasted good, and not like
the death you've heard about your whole life,
the one at fifty, the one in the 1970s,
your name was her name before it was yours
and it never would have been
if she didn't leave it behind.

Genesis, Suburbia

Lake water, dune grass.
Interstate overpass. Chicago Skyway

Toll Booth lit up in neon,
that road to a future

where the Jetsons drive in domes
and I count the giraffe necks

of lampposts until I reach one hundred
or give up, three years old, bored

with infinity. The three March days
in '98 the sky drops fifteen inches

of snow, my sister and I scattering
sunsets across the carpet, puzzle pieces

like flat candy corn. Each night
we sleep like caterpillars in sleeping bags

by the fireplace until the power
surges back, the house aglow

with epiphanies. Tire tracks
in cornfields. A June night a deer

leaps across the gravel in front of our car.
Bridging the chasm of the two corn-stalked worlds

on either side of us, I swear
I hear the thin bones of her legs

bounding toward us in the second before
we scream. Kite in the trunk.

Viking face stenciled green
on a white water tower. Dog-walkers

at dawn. Plastic swans on the ponds.
Organ pipes, wooden pews.

Jordan's Bulls. *Chicago Tribune*. Christmases
in Evergreen Park, the checkerboard floor

of my aunt's kitchen, my cousins
and uncles twisting their mouths into James Stewart,

one thought bubble above us imagining
George Bailey sprinting through snow

after jumping off a bridge, so ever since I was six
we celebrate Christmas

while referencing suicide. Heavy sound
of trains on track miles away.

Mean Girls. Tina Fey. Five-cent
thrift store Frisbee my friends throw

down the senior-class hallway. August nights
toilet-papering trees, mixed CDs,

quarter-moons. Yearly springtime
dogwood bloom. Popcorn

in the afternoon. Rocks like fists
hurled into ponds, drumbeat

plunge to the bottom. Bonfires. Charred
autumns. Fireworks shot

like neurons into the night's synapses
where thoughts dissolve / scatter. A glass of wine

with my parents on their deck.
When I stand too fast—

coneflowers explode, a pink
nova—my foot kicks over the glass

and it shatters.

les(bi)an

The spring I could say aloud
to myself, *I like girls*, I was twenty,
listening to Ani DiFranco,
watching *The L Word*, reading
on Taoism before bed
by flashlight. On every page
a photograph of rocks or trees,
mountains, flowing water.
That semester I wrote poems
and watched *Planet Earth*.
Meanwhile, Saturn
with her belted halo
of ice, spun on.

Window Seat Arithmetic

Subtract the need to arrive
at an answer and add four cornfields
divided by a crossroads.

Take away the cows. Sun.
Substitute the moon. Near Illinois,
cancel out the Indiana Dunes.

Add rust. Steel silhouette of Chicago.
Clack-clack of the L snaking 'round the Loop
and long Amtrak rail running south
to New Orleans. Take away

the quiet of the train
and add a father calling
his daughter to say

he's proud. Their conversation passes
like barns. Glassy reflections of clouds
cloak your face in wind.

clavicle sympathy pains

how you hear
the paper
of a joint burning

how she said
or was it
the idea of her
that said

two people
can be two pages
of one book

that we come
from mucus membranes

that a body
can be a moment
of silence

a pencil
writes the letter
'd' over
and over

like a bricklayer
building
a hard wall
around
what's soft

history tells us
our sadness
is not new

we live in mansions
of categories

I am of a people
called Capricorn

ruled by Saturn
a hula-hoop
circles my feet
like a ring of salt

I am thinking
of the fantasies
of trees

one relationship
I've given myself
fully to
is my cell phone

flat rectangular eye

it gets all of me

the symbol
for Capricorn is a goat
with a fish tail

I draw my body on paper
and see a matchstick
you could strike

Why I Shouldn't Be an FBI Special Agent

Friends, today on this rainy April afternoon,
while searching the job boards of the internet,
cup of coffee near my hands hovering
above the alphabet, I learned I could apply
to be a Special Agent for the FBI.
And before you think I'm fucking with you
I fit all the requirements. Bachelor's Degree.
Driver's License. Right age range. I'm a
U.S. citizen that's been working for at least thirty-six months.
It's all there. And they even try to sell it too.
Say how every day's different. An ongoing investigation
in the morning. Testify at court before lunch. As if
I'm going to apply to the FBI purely for the wide net
of pace-changing experiences, as if they know
everyone is distracted these days,
that we need constant stimulation or else we dissolve
into a pool of red salt. And I'd be lying if I said
I'm not considering it. I'm a poet, after all.
What if there's an X-Files type gig lurking in my future
and I never get to write all those extraterrestrial poems
inside me because I felt pressured to "stay in my field."
These are questions worth considering.
I'd probably be required to carry a gun,
and I'd probably be expected to use it, which
I do not want. The only time I've ever fired a gun
was in a cornfield in southern Illinois near the confluence
of the Ohio and Mississippi on the first of November
a few years back. An accordion player
with dreadlocks and a Robert E. Lee tattoo on his stomach
was in town for a show. A friend of the girl
I was into at the time, we all went to get bagels after beers
from Winston, the old man with the bagel cart
who loved shoveling carbohydrates to drunken college students.

We talked about the guns in his trunk, and because
I was curious, and because it felt like an experience
I needed to have, and because I thought
it could maybe impress her, before we knew it,
we were in the next town over, the cold metal heavy
in my hand, and me aiming the barrel
into the quiet nothingness of that field.
I fired twice. Once straight ahead, the second cocked
a little higher. The next morning, I woke up, panicked
that the bullet strayed through a window,
found a home in an old woman that couldn't sleep,
who was reading the paper and drinking tea
at her kitchen table. Or that it greeted an older man
getting out of his pick-up truck. Or that it found a dog.
The next few days I kept checking the local news
for stories about mysterious gun deaths, and thanked
whatever higher power I needed to every time I found nothing.
Which only means nothing got reported.

Which is to say, in another universe, the bullets
never landed, that they're still flying, defying
the laws of physics and gravity on a trajectory around
the planet, making small Saturns of the Earth.
Those bullets that sped away like two drag racers,
like fireworks exploding in my hands
with the small balls of cotton in my ears,
the way this girl always made me want
to try new things even though she stayed behind
the wheel the entire time
and the next week I got my first tattoo
of the symbol for pi on my left wrist,
which is to say circles, which is to say diameters,
which is to say the bullets never landed,
that I can't scrounge the dirt for the heaviness of lead
to weigh down my palms. Gravity doesn't apply
to the imagination. If I'm hollow on the inside,
just two bullets in a lake of air, it's because

I believed a gun could give me love. It's because
I grew up white in middle-class America with the idea
of violence but not violence. Which is to say
the mind can justify anything. Even this poem.

infinity tunnel: haiku

this is what you get
when you hold a mirror to
another mirror

Marble

Love, show me your teeth.
Show me the night settling

like a black pond, moon
a glint in a wolf's eye. Show me
your eyes of bone-white

and shadow, the bonfires
that stripped off our bark

and your throat full of bees.
Look. The river changes tenses
and I can't get enough of this

light, the needlework of stars
and the dozen broken hearts

it took to get to this one—
a marble peering through ashes
like moonlight in mist.

Self-Portrait as a Jack-o'-Lantern

This Halloween, call me
the New Legend of Sleepy Hollow
and carve my pumpkin head
into whatever you wish.
Wanna carve a dick? Fuck.
You wanna draw attention
to the red way the patriarchy glows? Sun-
shine, be my guest. It's nearing that
hallowed time, and what I'm saying is
make black triangles of my eyes and nose
or stencil me into a Disney princess
or the silhouette of an alley cat
or get meta with the whole thing:
a pumpkin inside a pumpkin until you're in
that other pumpkin patch of your mind
where yellow leaves ride wind
like surfboards in sun—there, too, I want you
to tear the corn stalks from the dirt
and raze and harvest the field. I want you
to hold the earth in your hands
and praise the dry riverbeds
of your cracked fingers, and when you say
Trick or Treat, motherfucker—
this is the trick: this is my skull
you're reaching into elbow-deep
grabbing seeds by the fistful.
This is my noggin you're tricking
into some funk-induced squash show.
I mean it. Start fresh
on this spongy canvas. Classic
mountain range mouth? Place me
on your porch stoop. Look
into the void of this vegetable.

Stick a candle inside my mouth,
light it, and step back.
I was born to glow
in the orange October dark.

Would You Rather Sonnet

I have grown cynical. Not cyclical
though that too: moving from relationship
to relationship, like my mom posting
a video of the sun on the lake.

Something about this moment feels braided
with belief systems. Mango pits, flowers
on flat horizons. Birds. Each star is a
pin prick stitching cold light and breath. Tonight

I realized I'd rather freeze to death than
burn. Like lying down for a nap that ends
not being a nap. Am I wrong? Besides,
I don't see it as a passionate door

to exit through anyway. Just the flames.
So orange and red and what they do to us.

RV Nation

Gallup, New Mexico

Friends, I want an RV. I mean, I really do.
Not one of those trailers you tack to the back
of a pickup either, but a semitruck sized
beauty, with a bald eagle, or the Grand Canyon
painted on the side. One with a flat screen
and coffee maker, board games, a bed for the dog
I'd walk with through the Redwoods,
a small awning to seek shade under, where I can wave
to my wandering clan. Because as I sit here
at a picnic bench jotting down retirement dreams
in this Americana Paradise of an RV park off Route 66
near the Arizona border, where an American flag
flattens the bottom of an empty swimming pool,
I feel my spirit here in the Southwest shift into reverse
and head back through the rocky contours of New Mexico
toward Oklahoma and Missouri. Back toward the basketball courts
of Friday night gyms in Indiana with soft pretzels
and blue raspberry slushies that froze each tongue and set of lips
into arctic trenches. The dirtiest kids at my school
would always ask, *why'd you give that Smurf*
a blowjob? And I suppose the best answer
would have been of course to say
because this is America, and I am free
to paint my body full of roses and call myself
a garden. I can pilgrimage to San Francisco and kneel down
to kiss the front steps of Danny Tanner's full house,
or visit a museum about the development of the atomic bomb
during the Second World War and learn about biofuels
and algae and note how the green color
always makes me think of the slime
Nickelodeon poured on everyone in the '90s,
which is to say I'm a millennial and remember defining time

before the internet dialed into my life, a little before
the towers in New York fell, or the word "terror" enacted
a force field around my heart I doubt I'll ever tear apart.
This morning I'll cross into Arizona and buy a $5 Navajo blanket
in a small yellow shop shadowed
by a mountain of red rocks where
life-sized plastic horses and goats guard a wild space.
Friends, I can't help but love this country
and every outdoor public piano on it.
This morning, John behind the desk made coffee at 8 a.m.
and the bathrooms here are the cleanest bathrooms
I've ever seen, I mean, pristine
and I know my head is as scattered as sand
in a desert wind sometimes, but I've come here to this page
out of love, for every recreational vehicle
in this park, from the 1970s until now, how I pause
at each portrait of mountains and streams on tin panel,
how I discuss with the carved wood bears sunbathing
near the Statue of Liberty around this pool
everything I have to say
about the soul and all that this RV park
makes me feel, which is exactly
what art
is supposed to do.

Ode to The Weather Channel

Nation covered in cloud. Million acres
drenched in rainwater. Saturated

with something you could call love. If you want.
Because today at 5:17, the Doppler showed me a green

Indiana, meaning it rained. Not over Ohio
or Illinois, but for at least one second

only Indiana, her flag of blue
and yellow stars. Outside, the air felt thick.

Dirt became 75 percent water
so we are more alike than I thought

and another warm front arrived from the West,
which may have something to do

with the 311 tornados already this spring,
and tomorrow that number will rise

like floodwaters in Missouri and Arkansas. Still, there is warmth
because it is seventy-six degrees right now in Madrid

where I have a friend who I imagine is happier today
than he was yesterday when it was fifty-two. And yes.

I am aware this heat stretching the globe
is not completely desirable. I am aware of this

when I slide my feet into sandals. Instead
I like to recall the giant globe spinning

on the ground floor of the largest building on my college campus
at a rate of rotation so quick, it leaves you standing still

to watch one day pass in fifteen minutes. If you want
you can even pretend you're the sun

though you should be aware
you will burn out in about four billion years

so no, this life will not last, but thank goodness for the button
on the wall next to this earth whose sign reads:

Press Button
To Hesitate
Revolution

so for once, we can stop
where we are, still

in this space, and listen to the rain
tap the window like static, and not worry

that there are still dishes to clean,
vegetables to eat, and clothes to change.

I'd like to tell someone this. The next person
walking by perhaps with a song in their ears.

I want to get their attention, watch their finger
press the pause button in the middle of some refrain

so I can show them this sign, waiting for the moment
on their face that says *I understand*.

I want to do this. And then watch
that same finger press that same button

to start everything magical
moving once again.

Self-Portrait as Loan Payment

When I create the account to pay off my college loans,
part of the process tells me to choose an image

that mirrors my identity, so whenever I log in
the internet will show me myself: spiral-shaped

Shell like our infinite nature, Pirate Ship,
Guy in a Top Hat because every now and then

we should get a little classy. Four pages of this.
Racecars and Power Drills side by side. Dog jumping

a fence. Piano with the lid propped open like a skull flap
during brain surgery. Showgirl. Soldier. Seahorse. Sunset. Da Vinci's

Vitruvian Man in between the plastic pink face of a Ken Doll
and a Stapler. I know a white guy made this list too

because the woman in the third row wearing red lipstick
is simply labeled "Woman," whereas the "Scholar" is a white man

in glasses. Moments, too, I think an existential crisis
could occur—the cartoon hand pointing to a clock

in the next box, pearled glaze of an eyeball, bridge connecting Liberty
with Butterflies. How could I choose just one?

Am I not the exoskeleton of a Beetle, the sour face of a Frog?
I want to be half-Rooster, half-Waterfall. One-third Rubber Duck,

two-thirds box of Crayons. I know my mother would pick the box
with Cake, but me—I don't know. Mornings I've preferred the red flash

of a Cardinal on gray sky, others the shining silver wrists
of Wrenches. Yesterday I bought a Knitted Hat.

I could pick the Waltz, a Magician, or a Boxing Match but before I
     choose the skull
and crossbones of a Pirate Flag, reasoning Death is like

the one true thing, the buttons linking to the previous and next pages
freeze, so I'm left with Michelangelo, Mona Lisa, the seahorse,

or Barbie's BFFL (Boyfriend for Life). I almost choose him
as an ironic nod to consumer culture

but instead click the black and white drawing of a girl waving
a feathered fan on her chest like a pharaoh or flapper. I can label it

whatever I want, so I write out the word "Loanzzzz" with four z's
like I've fallen asleep at the end of the alphabet

and hit "Complete" where I'm taken to a screen that says
my next payment will be due in twenty-nine days.

Ode to Graph Paper, or Questions for the Cardinal

Little squares   cross hatch   checkerboard   black and white

tile floor   laid out   in quadrants   double axes

intersections   I love   how you cross   perpendicular

like that, love   90 degree   angles, right   elbow bent

palm running   parallel   to trees   saying Yes

you rise   roots witness   to rain   limbs reaching

from columns   listening   to quiet   equations

wooden monks   chanting   to a girl   a rose

inked in black   on her spine   centered   in numbered

coordinates   the bloom   plotted   (0,0), which

does not   translate into   two nothings   next to another

on a train   but the place   where negative   meets positive

space   where breath   threads through   earthy fabrics

bones build   adobe   and a red   gymnast bird

hops back   and forth on   electrical wire   drawn like

pencil lines   through sky—   O   little wingspan

little horizon   fluttering   in air   were you there

when woman rose vertical to face the sea? Was it

a night like this little bird a moon

like this when you stitched to blue quilt of sky?

Does a song rise and fall according to its slope? Tell me.

Do the notes move, left to right, like beads inside your throat?

Specialization: Early 2000s

Decades from now,
in a college history course
about the early twenty-first century,
yearly ritual of roses
on *The Bachelor*, an era
when TV cameras X-rayed
the ordinary heart, there will be
lectures on Trump, the search
for the right apprentice
academically comparable
to Darth Sidious, and some
will watch those debates
and laugh, but this isn't about that.
No, more and more, I see our planet
alone in the universe like a sad kid

not fitting in to the recess
gravity gave him. I subtract God and confess
I believe we're left to figure out
this one for ourselves. Every day
there's a new graphic about what
the new coastlines will be
once the sea swallows Miami.
America, when you catch yourself
in glass windows on the sidewalk,
what percentage of your perception
is denial? I drive your roads
and watch a Unitarian sun set behind mountains.
I believe in the prickly pear cactus
which is only to say I saw it once,
and it exists without me. The only time
I've ever been to a mountaintop
was in Taos, New Mexico,
where I smoked a bowl and looked out

at the deep gash of the Rio Grande carving
the landscape like a heartbreak.
I am all rock and gorge
and a river sidewinds through me
at shallowly depths.
I am akin to fire before tears.
I suspect history will mostly be video series and memes
and too much information. They might say
we were overwhelmed. They might
determine we didn't have enough power
to process it all.

House Rules

Upon entry, all Aquarians must sign
a metaphorical waiver. All Scorpios
must listen with a deep, concentrated
experience of time. If you ever find
yourself snapping out of a trance, write
three affirmations to muscle memory
and fire. The woods behind the house
belong to winter. Excuse me while I match
my breathing with the soil. Irish monks
used to pray with their palms up
like their hands were garden beds,
like a rose bush could rise from a saucer
of skin. Please note the birdhouses
on the windows, the shadow snuggling light.
Be sure to stand inside the circle beneath
the chandelier of elk antlers I found by the river.
Somewhere I have hidden a key. Find it
then find the door it opens. Hint: do not
overlook the liminal space between summer
and fall. Here is a portrait of Dennis Rodman,
the first anti-hero I ever loved. I was going
for tattooed grace. I was going for offensive
rebounds. Until I breathed the air
in the Upper Peninsula of Michigan,
I never understood the phrase
frog's in your throat, which says more
about me, but we can't always control
who we are. If you build a fire, please do so
in the designated stone circle with rocks
from the Great Lakes. At this desk, come up
with the plural form of your given name.
More than one of me is a Tradition.
Here is the piano and drums. No one else
is here yet. I'm so happy you came.

Glendalough

County Wicklow, Ireland

Story goes, one morning, the sun, an orange eye
above the hills, St. Kevin held out his hand in the mist

    and a bird rooted in his open palm.

Built a nest from birch twigs. Laid three eggs.
For months Kevin stood like stone. Statue awaiting the birth

    of wings. Today, limestone crosses erode. Each name

scratched into gravestone has been scoured away by wind
as lichen crawls up the church rock, and the far away spray

    of waterfall a half-mile up the hiking trail.

Weeks earlier, while driving the back roads near Bloomington, Indiana,
the night exhaled honeysuckle. I watched a boy I didn't know

    play guitar beneath pineapple lights strung above a backyard.

I couldn't look away. Staring deeper and deeper into that moment
the boy burst into flower petals. In two years, I have fallen in love

    a thousand times, my heart a hot air balloon inflating

in the high New Mexican desert until the seams split, balloon wrinkling
like bed sheets in sand. In the brochure I learn the Round Tower protected

    against Viking invaders. Each time it collapsed, monks

rebuilt it using the original sixth-century stone. In the monastery today,
wind dusting the trees, I begin to hear something. As if my body were old

and near to the grave. As if I had reached

the birch tree tunnel's end, bumblebee buzzing in the dogrose,
Glen of Two Lakes whispering of when the glacier slid aside, I hear

the angel the story says led St. Kevin to this land stuck in the wind

like flute song. The angel knows this land like the gray heron knows her reflection
on the water. Silver plumage shimmering. My mind wandering home.

When the angel asks where I come from, I say from a heart attack.

Two chicken tacos. An iPod's murmur through a fuzzy car stereo.
Say girl-crushes and late-night skinny-dipping, Lake Michigan before a ranger

told us to put our clothes on, go home. A place called the Valley

of Paradise, where corn grew like foxglove by the old Froberg home
off Rollercoaster Road where teen drivers tested fate and dark hills.

Say Labrador puppies. Empty parking lots. The electricity

of lips, and a boy I loved without ever knowing his story.
I say there's a castle around my heart. I'm ready to not be ready.

That two nights before I flew to this country, after I fell from a tree

in a beer garden, after a picnic table branded me in blood, I met a woman parked
in a Nissan beneath the haloed light of the bar's parking lot lamppost.

She asked me, though I hadn't said a word:

Are you leaving America in two days? I say I have looked at the world
through the eyes of someone about to leave it. That the previous summer

my friend's dad died. I brought him Mexican food

afterward in a brown paper bag. That the world we grew up in
was already gone.

Off the path—a patch of purple aster. I follow it

to the waterfall. Listening to the white noise grow louder,
finally I stand next to it. My heart a basket of static.

Poem Wearing a Party Hat

Tonight my hands kaleidoscope.
Stretched back, two slingshot eyes
ready to laser a marble block
into a sculpture of the Pacific along
California's October coast. I ask:
what isn't lost in translation?
I'd like a redwood tree
to defend me in a court of law.
I forget is the new *Amen*.
Look it up, the body of Christmas.
Excuse me, but every third Wednesday
the night sky royally fucks me
like my body's a spaceship
on a Southwestern rug just before
the evening settles down
into an aquarium
of radical ideas. Now
I have a taste for drought.
This Halloween, the Backstreet Boys
will rise again and the shrimp
in the Chesapeake Bay
will choreograph their interpretation
of the end times. Somewhere
a desert town's fossilizing
and the future's being foretold
in .gifs and drone selfies, but I can't wait
for the Year of the Barnyard
when true love will ride in
saddled to ostriches, or the Year
of the Hammock when the wind
will control everything, especially
the Great Lakes. I was born
in the Year of the Compost Pile,

which explains my predisposition
for recycling my thoughts and emotions,
but my sister was conceived
in the Year of the Search Engine,
so there's always an algorithm in the air
between us, the way people once said
love was, or spring. If you need me,
just call me by my scientific
name. I'll be standing by
downloading the new software
into my fingers under a ceiling
of umbrellas, glossing through
this Age of Imaginary Genies.

The Sweatshirt, 2005

for Brandy

When you plant your nose
to the cotton, smell the smoke.

Cornfields after 10 p.m.
Night before I left.

Put your nostrils to the neckline
digging deeper than detergent

until you hit how my skin smelled
that summer: cold sand, a sunrise.

Don't be afraid to push your arms
through the sleeves. To lift your head

through the hole. To fill the space
where my ribs and lungs once knew

the name for warmth. Do this. Cross
your arms and look up—past the satellites

and depths of outer space, into another
night, and smell there. Oxygen

thinning. Void without redwood or farm.
Inhale the sweetness of hydrangea

and do not think of the distance
between a body and her heaven.

Look at your arms. Stained white.
Green lettering spelling *Lady Vikes*

across your chest. Smell this
other body. When your eyeglasses

break or it hurts too much
to touch the kettle on the stove,

when your tongue won't deliver the words
needing to be said, put your face

to the dirt and breathe. Smell.
When our bodies come back,

I'll want them to remember this scent.

Elegy for Seth Cohen from The O.C.

Your pool house is a funeral now. Maybe that's harsh
but so was when you sailed your boat to Tahiti

and next season had to be rescued from Luke's house in Portland
after they moved because his dad was gay, and you know, I don't even know why

I care to be honest. You loved Summer Roberts, and like, I loved Summer Roberts,
and wasn't that enough? What about when Marissa Cooper died?

What did you and Ryan do again, and where is Ryan now?
Why did you introduce me to so much music, with your sweater vests

and Southern California skateboarding on the pier? Seth Cohen—
I want to leave you at the party. I want the bonfire to take me back

in time and solve every angsty problem with Death Cab.
So many nights on Indiana roads, mist on the earth's breath.

I kept the windows all the way down. I could smell the dew on the flowers,
I breathed all of it in. What deals did you make with your dead?

I wish we could have seen you visit the Bronx with Sandy,
that's where the real stories were. Just like when I went to California

and leaned into every keyboard no matter the vacant music. Everything you are
is a ghost I've never quite shook. I don't know how many cornfields I've driven by,

how many gas station managers I've handed my debit card to in exchange
for an egg sandwich and coffee. You are 10,000 years ago. I only think of you now

when I think about Rachel Bilson and Bill Hader dating, how they were last seen
in Tulsa, Oklahoma, over the holidays, and maybe you only bother me

because it's been love this whole time. You, safe, my California
dream, then Marissa kissed Olivia Wilde and my tongue swelled

a small rainbow. I know it's good where you are—in Orange County,
hometown of the last new girl I started working with in wilderness therapy.

I was packed to leave the day she arrived. I don't know why, like me,
she'd come to Wisconsin in the middle of winter. Everyone I know

has grown up. I love the cold, I don't know anymore.
I can't tell if I miss you or there's a seagull nearby.

Four Poets, a Bicycle, and a Walk through an Empty Parking Lot

Click-click of gears keep time.
Distant traffic. Morning language

of doves. I know
I won't pass this way again

for a long while, so I try
absorbing everything: rows

of sunflowers
in my friend's garden.

The grown and wild grass.
Bee sucking nectar

from a snapdragon,
but I'm already somewhere else

words can't touch.
Side by side with this green Schwinn,

step after step through space
after space, I attempt to construct

a philosophy for goodbye.
In three weeks, I'll cross an ocean.

In ten months almost to the day,
in a hospice center

in Florida, my grandpa will pass away
while my sister sketches

in colored pencil
her vision of the lake

by his house with a note
my mother would deliver

in person that afternoon, except
she got the news around 2 a.m.

that he died, and her plane took off
without her. In the morning,

I'll walk to her room, climb
into her bed, and she'll say

he always wanted his grandchildren to have
early memories of the water

but none of that
has happened yet in this wide-

open parking lot I walk through
with three friends. My tires turn

in synchronization
with every thought I don't allow

into my throat or past
my teeth. A squirrel runs

the length of a power line. The sun's
one of many stars. And I walk

into the street with my bike,
my shadow a body of wheels.

moonkite: haiku

moon from the backseat
    silver ball at the end of
        invisible string

Cognitive Function

Late February, northern New Mexico.

Kitchen table color of cream, paint
scratched off after years of breakfasts.

Through the window, snow
blankets everything. In this town,

more art galleries than restaurants.
Mountains on all sides. Pink and lavender
sunsets on snowy peaks.

I learn what I can from stillness.
Orange glow of candles in paper bags.

Whatever light lives
in the approaching darkness, recently
I read hope is a cognitive
function and I can't stop
thinking about it.

On the table, a plastic bear leans forward,
doubled-over at the gut.
All the honey rushed to its head.

Moonrise Ritual

Fill a tub with saltwater
and soak your feet for one hour.

Write an apology to the dinosaurs
on behalf of outer space.
Breathe harmonica. Imagine
sleeping in an igloo of sand.

A crow perches on a rainbow.
A satellite photographs the thirty-seventh second
of a pie-eating contest.

There's still time to paint your nails
the color of lava or dirt.

A guitar could have been paper.
Folded correctly, paper blooms into lotus.

When the hour is finished,
smell your feet for traces
of ocean.

Do not dry off with a towel.

Run to the nearest school or bank
and string a bed sheet up the flagpole.

Pulling the rope toward you, raise
this new banner to wind—mud
between toes, fabric of sleep

rippling like waves, heart drumming
beneath the calm of your hand—

and pledge allegiance
to the tempo of the tides.

Poem Ending with Fantasy of Building a Bonfire

Dear music that makes me think of
        queer spaces and elegant

line breaks: I just learned that each
        of the 1,600 suckers of a giant Pacific octopus

can taste like our tongues taste, and sometimes
        music is so sexy I want to make love

to an entire room of strangers with only
        my eyes, but this is a dream, isn't it?

I swivel my ass on a chair and overhear
        a conversation between two dads—

one drinking a blonde ale with likely his first
        newborn on the table, his left hand

on the baby's belly, while the other,
        older dad, dark-haired and white

and I'm gonna guess in his forties, seems to be
        looking to walk a trail back into a past life.

This is not a publicly queer space, but
        the music in my head sings otherwise.

Dads aside, God bless the drag queens, synthesizers,
        and pop music of Christina Aguilera.

God bless the ways we pass or don't because
        I get tired, and we should probably just bless them.

Before I ever held a vocabulary that included *gender*
        or *queer,* I learned that to be Midwestern

was to fit inside a narrow alley between
        the East and West Coasts. If I could distill

my mind, you'd know that what turns me on
        is occasionally bizarre and strange, photo-

synthetic, but who are we kidding? Octopuses
        snake their bodies through the oceans, and I

just learned it is *octopuses,* not *octopi*
        because you can't add a plural "i," which is Latin,

to a Greek word, like *octopus.* I feel like there's a Catholic
        part of me that needs to apologize

for this, and for everything we've done
        and are doing. I'd like to be as carefree

as the little white girl skipping through this
        northern Minnesota taproom, but I've lived that

life already. I don't want to get lost imagining
        borders, my brain plunged

in personless policies, so maybe we could just
        touch each other instead? Whoever you are,

even if it's only in my mind. I need you
        to know, I feel like good whiskey.

        And like birch, I burn instantly.

At the Twilight of the Big Bang

> We live at the end of an era. We live in one of those
> singular moments in history when one scientific and
> culturally accepted concept of cosmic origins is fading
> and others, yet unproven, vie for ascendency.
> —Adam Frank, physicist, NPR

Not a bullet's discharge
from the chamber—

   atomic shrapnel.

Even now, the world uncurls
      in fern, says *yes*
to lilac and eucalyptus. Once

it was new. Night sky.
     Skulls full of stars.

The Big Bang—named like
      a human names

     a goldfish.
New theory: all theories decay

      in time, so why not
      name it

again? Birth of bumblebee and
nerve: fields unfold

        in a big bloom

The Crickets Remember

These days, any little thing
distracts me. Moth clicking
its torso on the tin roof
in Morse code. Red drops
of cranberry juice. Translucent
tote bag placed over
the white halogen light burning
on my balcony. I forget what
pulled me outside to begin with.
Lack of walls, perhaps.
Or the faded howl of dogs.
Whatever it was, I'm worried
about the atmosphere again.
Once I wrote a Wikipedia entry
on the wind songs of the dead.

Tomorrow I'll suck the juice
from an orange, and a girl will place
a peanut shell into my palm, as she says,
everything vanishes into cloud
to return via the faucet in the bathroom
sink. Leaving Earth will be difficult
I think, but someone's mother
will make a lovely photo album
about it. My fortune cookie
never tells me I'm going to die.
It wouldn't be wrong.
In the desert, a motorcycle races
beneath a sky of horses
and bears. The crickets remember
September. In the dew-dropped grass
a girl climbs into the basket
of a hot-air balloon like she is diving
into a glass of lemonade.

These days, little makes sense
except the apples in my kitchen,
and the most restless trees
are Midwesterners. Even
if we don't survive the end
of the world, I hope the universe
reminds you of the night we drove
to the prison: my hands raised
through the moon roof, wind lacing
around my fingers. The songs
I don't know are my favorite.
My favorite language is the one
you speak in my ear
though I don't understand.

Poem for Ms. Frizzle

How could one not love the driver
of a magical bus? A bus that shrinks and spins

with the push of some buttons, the bus always—
and this is important—driven by lesbians:

Lily Tomlin, Kate McKinnon, how love
for the cosmos somehow equates

with love for the feminine, the scientific method
a blanket braided with love for the classroom

that is the world: gardens and rivers and ears,
stars and satellites in orbit, the lungs,

blood cells, stomach. You can travel
anywhere any time, hear a tyrannosaurus,

watch glaciers form, *be* light.
Ms. Frizzle, Ms. Frizzle.

You know everyone. It's the joke. Everyone's
your friend, but we know so little about you.

Your companion, a green lizard.
And as of 2019, there are two Frizzes:

professor, a PhD, and an elementary school teacher
in a building with almost no other students.

Ms. Frizzle—and maybe I am talking
to McKinnon now—I think I love you. Could

love you. I know it's silly, you're a cartoon. Maybe
I just wish to hover above a sound wave,

a lunar crater, a rainforest. Maybe I wish my limbs
would convert into wind-blown seeds

so I could helicopter down into soil. You can tell me
everything you know about igneous rock,

the greenhouse effect on Venus, the impact
of the worldwide web on all of us. Say we can explore

and connect with those we don't know
like never before. Say it while some revelatory

soundtrack plays as you float in your space suit
with a student above the Pacific. How beautiful

your belief becomes there, and all that feeling in
your own heart: a flower, an ocean, a forest, an orchard.

tree hugger

so what is it
about circumference
when hugging a tree?
the diameter a line
straight through
time + back again,
starting + ending
in the present? what's
at the core anyway?
a handful of seventh graders
on an april morning years ago
planting a seed on earth day, or
setting a ball of roots into
the soil? research has shown
if a human gardens

or buries their own hands in the dirt—
not a literal burial, not
a grief at all—the brain spills
the confetti of oxytocin
all over the city streets of the body.
the brain / the body / the mind
doesn't know any better—
it assumes this digging
is like the bond between lovers, or
what happens in a new mother
in the first seconds she rocks
her baby. give me a number
greater than zero, any
old integer, + divide it by 3.14
+ on into forever, + you'll get
this line from present
to present, which is
a bond, which is, somehow, you + me

sharing this moment, a tree
off in some woods
on a mountain, scraping
the winter off its limbs, devouring
sunlight, the circumference
a wooded ripple
you could walk up to + reach
your arms all the way 'round

Embodied

Body of maps. Body of bones
and blood. Body of banjos,
lullaby, and lace. Body of nerve

and the taste of cinnamon.
Body of *let's begin again*.
Body of snowstorm and pinecone,

cordless phones, extension ladders.
Ice shelves, watersheds. Oxygen,
amphibious breath. Incense,

church bells, candle wax, *time
will tell*, timpani drums and
pterodactyl wings. Subway trains,

piano keys. Records rotating
like Neptuned jazz. Body of Polaroids
and alley cats. A pixilated

heart. Coral reefs, desert cars, oceans
mopping the shores. Body of blackbirds
in winter sky. Body of a billion

eyes, spacebars, fingerprints
of tree rings, the synonyms
for *everything*. Body of rivers

and blinking lights, TV screens,
silver, magenta. Body of rhymes
and placenta, the enter key

and mud-brick walls. Body
of brushstrokes and shifting jaws.
Memories of ostriches, the smells

of dirt, oil, monsters. Rusty song
of industry. Clank of tanks,
artillery. Drone strikes and sonar

echo. Waxy green of needled pine.
Body of pendulums, valentines,
interstates, words like stalactites

in my mouth's cave. Puddles
of orange juice in molars.
Dark rooms with skeletons

sitting in circles, Kleenex boxes,
rainbow necklaces of yarn. Body
of nails and barns and nirvanas. Once-

upon-a-times of trauma. Birthdays
etched into stone, volcanoes,
lanterns. The hymn

of numbers, repeating patterns.
Plastic. Seven forty-seven descending
through cloud. Cross left

to rot in the rain. Body of midnight
trains and sorrows. Body
of the wild tomorrow. Body

of a breath so borrowed.
Body of whistles and lime, stitches
and kisses, the stoplight sublime, this

body of tissue and pockets. This
body of turtle shell and flute.
Skin like peach glass and sun

rising off the roof, the end of May
and shifting dunes, beginning
of Yes and strict pull of a moon—

craters, projection of face, a rabbit,
I see you now—black sky, body
of polka dot and firefly. Once

I was a suitcase on a bus. Now
the calligraphy of a cornfield.
Opening like an envelope.

I am genetic code recalling
the first night years ago
when I burned like a book

and the stars organized themselves
like notes onto sheet music.
I am searching for ordinary

language. Translating rain. This
is a body of helicopter seeds.
No one can tell them not to dance.

swan hammer

before i fall asleep
the girl who lives
inside me dangles
like a bat in a cave

when she speaks
her voice
a conveyor belt

lobster claw
tongue

before sleep
the girl inside me
hammers the wall
of my skull

light rides in
on a wave
of flat paper swans

she folds one
she folds another

she's trying to tell me
she knows the way out

ACKNOWLEDGMENTS

So much gratitude to the editors and readers of the following publications in which these poems, sometimes in different versions, first appeared:

The Adroit Journal—"Embodied"
Arsenic Lobster—"Seasonal"
Atticus Review—"Ode to Graph Paper, or Questions for the Cardinal"; "Poem for Whomever Hacked My Debit Card and Spent $150 at the Macy's in Alexandria, Virginia"; "The Crickets Remember"
Avatar Review—"The Sweatshirt, 2005"
BOAAT—"Self-Portrait as a Jack-o'-Lantern"
Cosmonaut's Avenue—"Poem for Ms. Frizzle"
Duende—"Roller Derby Night in Southern Illinois"
Dunes Review—"At the Twilight of the Big Bang"
GlitterMOB—"Self-Portrait as Loan Payment"
Great Lakes Review—"Day 1, December 22, 2012"; "Poem for My Downstairs Neighbor"
Hobart—"RV Nation"
The Indianapolis Review—"les(bi)an"
Josephine Quarterly—"Window Seat Arithmetic"
Jet Fuel Review—"Elegy for the Early 21st Century Hipster"
The Louisville Review—"Pi Day"
Moon City Review—"Why I Shouldn't Be an FBI Special Agent"
Mortar Magazine—"clavicle sympathy pains"
Nashville Review—"Would You Rather Sonnet"
New Plains Review—"Genesis, Suburbia"; "swan hammer"
Nightjar Review—"Dear Los Angeles"
pacificREVIEW—"Tomato Prayer"
Pittsburgh Poetry Review—"Poem Wearing a Party Hat"
Quiddity—"I remember Nashville, the dueling piano bar"
Radar—"Self-Portrait as Hammer"
RHINO—"iContact / Screens"
Rogue Agent—"Margaret"
Salt Hill—"tree hugger"
Southern Indiana Review—"Specialization: Early 2000s"
Stirring: A Literary Collection—"Glendalough"
Toad—"The Ghost of Robert Frost Visits"
Utter—"Moonrise Ritual"; "Ode to The Weather Channel"
Willow Springs—"House Rules"
Winter Tangerine—"Marble"
Yemassee—"Poem Ending with Fantasy of Building a Bonfire"
Yes, Poetry—"Four Poets, a Bicycle, and a Walk through an Empty Parking Lot"

The poem "Cognitive Function" appeared in *Casita Poems: An Anthology* from Jambu Press, featuring alumni poets of the Helene Wurlitzer Foundation in Taos, New Mexico.

The poem "Getting Lost in Gary, Indiana" was awarded a fellowship from the Luminarts Cultural Foundation.

Thank you to everyone at the Luminarts Cultural Foundation, the Barbara Deming Memorial Fund, the Helene Wurlitzer Foundation, Sundress Academy for the Arts, the Union League Club of Chicago Library, Monson Arts, Kimmel Harding Nelson Center for the Arts, the Hutton Honors College at Indiana University, and Denali National Park (may we meet in person on a future day) for all of your support of my writing. Thank you to the Departments of English and Religious Studies at Indiana University and the English Departments at Southern Illinois University Carbondale and the University of Mississippi for their rigor. Thank you to Abdel Shakur and Jenny Burdge-Patel for my time at *Indiana Review* and everyone at *Crab Orchard Review*. Extra gratitude to the students and faculty of the MFA programs at SIUC and Mississippi: I feel so grateful and lucky to have crossed paths with you.

Special thanks to Ross Gay, Rodney Jones, Allison Joseph, Jon Tribble, Judy Jordan, Aimee Nezhukumatathil, Derrick Harriell, Beth Ann Fennelly, Melissa Ginsburg, Ann Fisher-Wirth, and Alyce Miller for your generosity and mentorship.

Thank you to Chris Mattingly, David Watters, and Ross Gay for all of the conversations and poems in Bloomington in the late 2000s. Forever grateful.

So much gratitude to everyone whose eyes, ears, hearts, minds, bodies, spirits spent time with many of these poems in earlier drafts, especially Brett Gaffney and Avery Guess. Additional gratitude to Judy, and to Allison and Jon for seeing something larger for "swan hammer."

So much of the reimagining of this collection occurred after my MFA in the context of my time living and working outside. Thank you to everyone at Camp McDowell and the McDowell Environmental Center in Alabama for the healing, the lessons in hands-on experiential learning, the canoeing, the enthusiasm, the love. I learned so much from all of you. Extra gratitude to Dan Paul for nudging me south and outside. Thank you to the Adams family and everyone at Emandal Farm for the bounty, the beauty, and the down-to-earth work. I'm so thankful for my time up near the redwoods and Pacific with y'all. Thank you to everyone at the Cahaba Environmental Center, the Cahaba River, and the Cahaba lily. I'm still trying to put all that beauty and wonder into words. Thank you to everyone at New Vision Wilderness for more than can possibly be mentioned here. Thank you to the students I worked with in Wisconsin and North Carolina for your courage, your vulnerability, your hearts, your humor. I think of you all often.

To my homeloves: Brandy Parker, Laura Coleman, Courtney Blomquist, Erica Johnson, Lisa Floran. Thank you for the laughter, for loving me, and for being a safe space back when we were babies. Thank you to my IU friends, especially Kelly Spicer for the deep talks. Thank you Dave Vettraino, Kevin Brody, and Brian Rovik for all you did, but especially for syncing the "Mountains" episode of *Planet Earth* to Radiohead's *Kid A*. I have only ever wanted to pass along that gospel, and now here I am, putting it in print. Thank you everyone who's ever played a sport with me. I appreciate you.

More gratitude: O-Jeremiah Agbaakin, Hussain Ahmed, Nadia Alexis, Ruth Awad, Stacey Balkun, Siobhan Barry, my high school poetry teacher Mrs. Berg, Ellie Black, Josh Bontrager, Armand Brint, Jessamine Chan, Alaina Clark, Emily Rose Cole, Bonnie Coleman, Kaci Darsow, Liz Deardorff, Fiskars, Aracelis Girmay, Siyun Fang, Leah Feldman, Jenny Flack, Loren Elise Foster, Ian Golando, Evan Hanover, Kim Hall, Erin Hansert, Winona Hapgood, Sadia Hassan, Kim Hommes, Brenda Johnson, Maggie Johnston, Devon Kelley-Yurdin, Jennifer Key, Nic Knight, Ben Koch, Jen Kopnicky, Austin Kodra, Tommy LeGrand, Marina Leigh, Kate Leland, Reba London, Zach Macholz, Phil Martin, Adrian Matejka, Andrew McSorley, Lucien Darjeun Meadows, Michael Meyerhofer, Michael Mlekoday, Heather Montgomery, Gabriel Mundo, Sequoia Nagamatsu, Joanna Ng, Joshua Nguyen, my elementary school speech therapist Mrs. Ogelsby, Reagan Payne, Noel Quiñones, Patrick Rosal, Laura Ruffino, Max Schleicher, Andy Sia, Ashley Sigmon, Carrie Sloan for gifting me your green Schwinn bicycle—thank you, Matthew Smith, Isaac Fletcher Weiss, Kevin Wilson, Mason Wray, and many more . . . everyone I've met at artist and writing residencies for the food and fellowship—thankful to have lived and made art alongside y'all. Thank you to everyone who's ever hosted me at an Airbnb. Thank you to WIUX Student Radio, Bloomington Bagel Company, the Boys & Girls Club of Porter County, and KidStop, Quatro's Pizza, Aladdin Pita on Rt. 30, NVW again, and all my co-guides, anyone who ever read my LiveJournal (long live), 9:07 C.H.U.D., the 2005 Chicago White Sox, Sufjan Stevens, the On Being podcast with Krista Tippett, that one dance party at Hannah's birthday party in 2012, the song "Holy" by Jamila Woods, Indiana Dunes National Park, forests, the night sky, dogs . . .

Thank you to Sarah Bagby for selecting this collection and making this dream come true. Thank you to Anita Skeen and everyone at the RCAH Center for Poetry, Wheelbarrow Books, and Michigan State University Press for the time, attention, and care you've put into turning these poems into a physical object that can exist in the world.

Big thank you to my aunts, uncles, cousins, and all of my extended Murphy and Graber families near and far for your love, support, conversations, hugs, memories, and laughter through all the seasons of this life. I am so happy to be yours.

To my parents: This book is dedicated to you. Thank you for all of your love and support—I love you [hugs]. And to my sibs, Matthew and Laura, I love you so gosh darn much.

In dearest memory of my grandparents, Jon Tribble, Dave Holloway, Kara Starr, and my uncle Tim Graber, among others.

And to you, dearest reader: thank you.

SERIES ACKNOWLEDGMENTS

We at Wheelbarrow Books have many people to thank without whom Maggie Graber's *Swan Hammer: An Instructor's Guide to Mirrors* would never be in your hands. We begin by thanking all those writers who submitted manuscripts to the tenth Wheelbarrow Books Prize for Poetry. We want to single out the finalists: Amber Adams, *Becoming Ribbons*; Anne Haven McDonnell, *Breath on a Coal*; Mary Ardery, *They're Not Lying When They Tell You You'll Dream of the Dead*; Catherine Prescott, *We Were Never Here*, whose manuscripts moved and delighted us and which we passed on to the final judge, along with Maggie Graber's manuscript, for her reading. That judge, Sarah Bagby, we thank for her thoughtful selection of the winner and her critical comments offered earlier in this book.

Our thanks to Lauren Russell, director of the RCAH Center for Poetry, for her support of Wheelbarrow Books, and to Laurie Hollinger, assistant director at the RCAH Center for Poetry, who also read manuscripts, along with Center for Poetry intern Jayla Harris-Hardy, and who provided the logistical aid and financial wizardry for this project. Sarah Teppen, a previous RCAH Center for Poetry intern, designed our Wheelbarrow Books logo which makes us smile every time we see it.

We thank Stephen Esquith, dean of the Residential College in the Arts and Humanities, who has given his continued support to the RCAH Center for Poetry and Wheelbarrow Books since our inception. As we began thinking seriously about Wheelbarrow Books, conversation with June Youatt, then provost at Michigan State University, was encouraging and MSU Press director Gabriel Dotto and former assistant director/editor-in-chief Julie Loehr were eager to support the efforts of poets to reach a hungry audience. We cannot thank them enough for having faith in us, and a love of literature, to collaborate on this project.

Thanks to our current Editorial Board, Sarah Bagby, Gabrielle Calvocoressi, Leila Chatti, Mark Doty, George Ellenbogen, Carolyn Forché, Thomas Lynch, George Ella Lyon, and Naomi Shihab Nye for believing Wheelbarrow Books a worthy undertaking and lending their support and their time to our success.

Finally, to our patrons: without your belief in the Wheelbarrow Books Poetry Series and your generous financial backing we would still be sitting around the conference table adding up our loose change. You are making it possible for poets who have never had a book of poetry published, something that's becoming harder and harder these days with so many presses discontinuing their publishing of poetry, to find an outlet for their work. You are also supporting the efforts of established poets to continue to reach a large and grateful audience. We name you here with great admiration and appreciation:

Beth Alexander   Mary Hayden
Gayle Davis   Patricia and Robert Miller
Fred Kraft   Brian Teppen
Jean Krueger

and candor of the arts and humanities to promote individual well-being and the common good. Students, faculty, and community partners in the arts and humanities have the power to focus critical attention on the public issues we face and the opportunities we have to resolve them. The arts and humanities not only give us the pleasure of living in the moment but also the wisdom to make sound judgments and good choices.

The mission, then, is to see things as they are, to hear things as others may, to tell these stories as they should be told, and to contribute to the making of a better world. The Residential College in the Arts and Humanities is built on four cornerstones: world history, art and culture, ethics, and engaged learning. Together they define an open-minded public space within which students, faculty, staff, and community partners can explore today's common problems and create shared moral visions of the future. Discover more about the Residential College in the Arts and Humanities at Michigan State at http://rcah.msu.edu.

WHEELBARROW BOOKS

Anita Skeen, *Series Editor*

Board

Sarah Bagby
Gabrielle Calvocoressi
Leila Chatti
Carol V. Davis
Mark Doty

George Ellenbogen
Carolyn Forché
Thomas Lynch
George Ella Lyon
Naomi Shihab Nye

Wheelbarrow Books, established in 2016, is an imprint of the RCAH Center for Poetry at Michigan State University, published and distributed by MSU Press. The biannual Wheelbarrow Books Poetry Prize is awarded every year to one emerging poet who has not yet published a first book and to one established poet.

SERIES EDITOR: Anita Skeen, professor emerita of the Residential College in the Arts and Humanities (RCAH) at Michigan State University, founder and past director of the RCAH Center for Poetry, director of the Creative Arts Festival at Ghost Ranch, and director of the Fall Writing Festival.

The RCAH Center for Poetry opened in the fall of 2007 to encourage the reading, writing, and discussion of poetry and to create an awareness of the place and power of poetry in our everyday lives. We think about this in a number of ways, including through readings, performances, community outreach, and workshops. We believe that poetry is and should be fun, accessible, and meaningful. We are building a poetry community in the Greater Lansing area and beyond. Our undertaking of the Wheelbarrow Books Poetry Series is one of the gestures we make to aid in connecting good writers and eager readers beyond our regional boundaries. Information about the RCAH Center for Poetry at MSU can be found at http://poetry.rcah.msu.edu and also at https://centerforpoetry.wordpress.com and on Facebook and Twitter (@CenterForPoetry).

The mission of the Residential College in the Arts and Humanities at Michigan State University is to weave together the passion, imagination, humor,